A Can-Do Attitude!

You Can Do It!

I0811906

Mitchell Allen

SOCIAL AND EMOTIONAL LEARNING FOR THE REAL WORLD™

Rosen Classroom™

What do you want to do?
Can you do it?

You can do anything.
You just need to believe it.

A can-do attitude is a tool.
Use it!

You want to make the school play. What can you do?

Use your can-do attitude.
Believe you can make it.

Practice your script.
It will take time.

What if you don’t succeed?
Try again!

Don't give up.
Keep your can-do attitude.

You will succeed!
It's time to make another goal.

Can you do it?
Yes, you can!

Words to Know

play

script